SP
611
KLI

6.1

3 4880 05000108 5
Klingel, Cynthia
Fitterer.

Skin = Piel

$10.46

DATE DUE	BORROWER'S NAME	ROOM NO.
9/9/4	Dal To,mjroj y	
		109

Let's Read About Our Bodies
Conozcamos nuestro cuerpo

Skin/Piel

Cynthia Klingel & Robert B. Noyed
photographs by/fotografías por Gregg Andersen

Reading consultant/Consultora de lectura: Cecilia Minden-Cupp, Ph.D.,
Adjunct Professor, College of Continuing and Professional Studies, University of Virginia

WeeklyReader.
EARLY LEARNING LIBRARY

For a free color catalog describing Weekly Reader® Early Learning Library's list of high-quality books, call 1-800-542-2595 or fax your request to (414) 332-3567.

Library of Congress Cataloging-in-Publication Data

Klingel, Cynthia.
    Skin = Piel / by Cynthia Klingel and Robert B. Noyed. — [Bilingual ed.]
      p. cm. — (Let's read about our bodies = Conozcamos nuestro cuerpo)
    Includes bibliographical references and index.
    Summary: A bilingual introduction to skin, what it is used for, and how to take care of it.
    ISBN 0-8368-3078-4 (lib. bdg.)
    1. Skin—Juvenile literature. [1. Skin. 2. Spanish language materials—Bilingual.]
    I. Title: Piel. II. Noyed, Robert B. III. Title.
    QM484.K565   2002
    611'.77—dc21   2001055094

This edition first published in 2002 by
Weekly Reader® Early Learning Library
330 West Olive Street, Suite 100
Milwaukee, WI 53212 USA

Copyright © 2002 by Weekly Reader® Early Learning Library

An Editorial Directions book
Editors: E. Russell Primm and Emily Dolbear
Translators: Tatiana Acosta and Guillermo Gutiérrez
Art direction, design, and page production: The Design Lab
Photographer: Gregg Andersen
Weekly Reader® Early Learning Library art direction: Tammy West
Weekly Reader® Early Learning Library page layout: Katherine A. Goedheer

Printed in the United States of America

4 5 6 7 8 9 10 09 08 07 06

Note to Educators and Parents

As a Reading Specialist I know that books for young children should engage their interest, impart useful information, and motivate them to want to learn more.

Let's Read About Our Bodies is a new series of books designed to help children understand the value of good health and of taking care of their bodies.

A young child's active mind is engaged by the carefully chosen subjects. The imaginative text works to build young vocabularies. The short, repetitive sentences help children stay focused as they develop their own relationship with reading. The bright, colorful photographs of children enjoying good health habits complement the text with their simplicity to both entertain and encourage young children to want to learn — and read — more.

These books are designed to be used by adults as "read-to" books to share with children to encourage early literacy in the home, school, and library. They are also suitable for more advanced young readers to enjoy on their own.

Una nota a los educadores y a los padres

Como especialista en lectura, sé que los libros infantiles deben interesar a los niños, proporcionar información útil y motivarlos a aprender.

Conozcamos nuestro cuerpo es una nueva serie de libros pensada para ayudar a los niños a entender la importancia de la salud y del cuidado del cuerpo.

Los temas, cuidadosamente seleccionados, mantienen ocupada la activa mente del niño. El texto, lleno de imaginación, facilita el enriquecimiento del vocabulario infantil. Las oraciones, breves y repetitivas, ayudan a los niños a centrarse en la actividad mientras desarrollan su propia relación con la lectura. Las bellas fotografías de niños que disfrutan de buenos hábitos de salud complementan el texto con su sencillez, y consiguen entretener a los niños y animarlos a aprender nuevos conceptos y a leer más.

Estos libros están pensados para que los adultos se los lean a los niños, con el fin de fomentar la lectura incipiente en el hogar, en la escuela y en la biblioteca. También son adecuados para que los jóvenes lectores más avanzados los disfruten leyéndolos por su cuenta.

Cecilia Minden-Cupp, Ph.D., Adjunct Professor,
College of Continuing and Professional Studies, University of Virginia

This is my skin.
It covers my body.

———————

Ésta es mi piel.
Me cubre el cuerpo.

My skin helps me stay warm when it is cold.

\- - - - - - -

Mi piel me ayuda a estar caliente cuando hace frío.

My skin helps me stay
cool when it is hot.

- - - - - - -

Mi piel me ayuda a
estar fresco cuando
hace calor.

Skin comes in many colors.

- - - - - - -

La piel puede ser de muchos colores.

My skin has freckles.
Freckles are fun!

Mi piel tiene pecas. ¡Las
pecas son divertidas!

I keep my skin clean.
I wash with soap
and water.

Mantengo mi piel
limpia. La lavo con
jabón y agua.

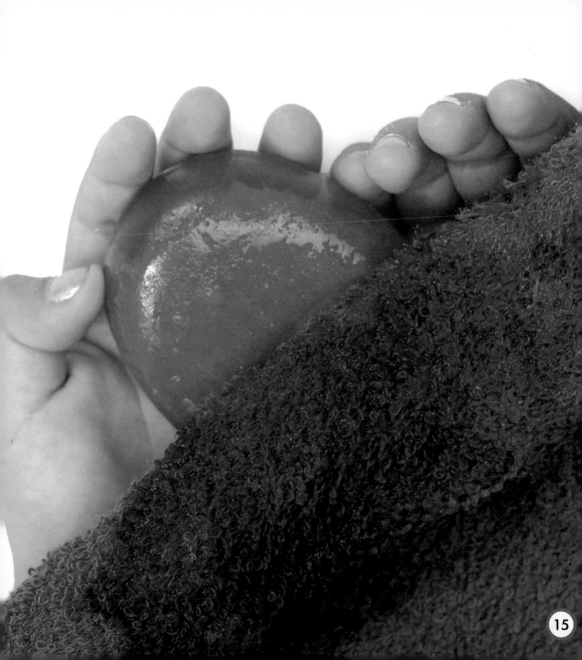

Too much sun can burn my skin. Sunscreen helps keep my skin safe.

Demasiado sol puede quemarme la piel. La protección solar me ayuda a cuidar la piel.

Sometimes I fall down and hurt my skin. My skin gets scraped.

A veces me caigo y me lastimo la piel. Me hago un rasguño.

A bandage helps me feel better. Thanks, Mom!

Una curita me ayuda a sentirme mejor. ¡Gracias, mamá!

Glossary/Glosario

bandage—a strip of cloth that covers a wound
curita—tira de tela que cubre una herida

freckles—small, brownish spots on the skin
pecas—pequeñas manchitas de color café en la piel

scraped—skin injured by something rough or sharp
rasguño—herida en la piel causada por algo áspero o afilado

sunscreen—a lotion or cream that protects the skin from the Sun
protección solar—loción o crema que protege la piel de las quemaduras del Sol

For More Information/Más información

Fiction Books/Libros de ficción
Machado, Ana Maria. *Nina Bonita: A Story.* Brooklyn, N.Y.: Kane/Miller Book Pub., 1996.

Messinger, Midge. *Freddie Q. Freckle.* Lake Hiawatha, N.J.: Little Mai Press, 1998.

Nonfiction Books/Libros de no ficción
Sandeman, Anna. *Skin, Teeth, & Hair.* Brookfield, Conn.: Copper Beech Books, 1996.

Showers, Paul. *Your Skin and Mine.* New York: Harper Collins Juvenile Books, 1991.

Web Sites/Páginas Web
Why Does My Skin Get Wrinkly in Water?
kidshealth.org/kid/talk/qa/wrinkly_fingers.html
For information about how your skin works

Index/Índice

About the Authors/Información sobre los autores

Cynthia Klingel has worked as a high school English teacher and an elementary school teacher. She is currently the curriculum director for a Minnesota school district. Cynthia Klingel lives with her family in Mankato, Minnesota.

Cynthia Klingel ha trabajado como maestra de inglés de secundaria y como maestra de primaria. Actualmente es la directora de planes de estudio de un distrito escolar de Minnesota. Cynthia Klingel vive con su familia en Mankato, Minnesota.

Robert B. Noyed started his career as a newspaper reporter. Since then, he has worked in school communications and public relations at the state and national level. Robert B. Noyed lives with his family in Brooklyn Center, Minnesota.

Robert B. Noyed comenzó su carrera como reportero en un periódico. Desde entonces ha trabajado en comunicación escolar y relaciones públicas a nivel estatal y nacional. Robert B. Noyed vive con su familia en Brooklyn Center, Minnesota.